Killer Snakes/Serpientes asesinas

Spitting Cobra/
Cobra escupidora

By Avery Willebrandt   Traducción al español: Eduardo Alamán

 **Gareth Stevens**
Publishing

Please visit our website, www.garethstevens.com. For a free color catalog of all our high-quality books, call toll free 1-800-542-2595 or fax 1-877-542-2596.

Library of Congress Cataloging-in-Publication Data

Willebrandt, Avery.
[Spitting cobra. Spanish & English]
Spitting cobra = Cobra escupidora / Avery Willebrandt.
    p. cm. — (Killer snakes = Serpientes asesinas)
Includes index.
ISBN 978-1-4339-5653-9 (library binding)
1. Spitting cobras—Juvenile literature. I. Title. II. Title: Cobra escupidora.
QL666.O64W5518 2011
597.96'42—dc22

                              2011012003

First Edition

Published in 2012 by
Gareth Stevens Publishing
111 East 14th Street, Suite 349
New York, NY 10003

Designer: Michael J. Flynn
Editor: Greg Roza
Spanish Translation: Eduardo Alamán

Photo credits: Cover, pp. 1, (pp. 2-4, 6, 8, 10, 12, 14, 16, 18, 20-24 snake skin texture), 5, 6-7, 9, 15 Shutterstock.com; pp. 11, 17 Tom Brakefield/Stockbyte/Getty Images; p. 13 Digital Vision/Getty Images; p. 19 iStockphoto; p. 21 Dave Hamman/Gallo Images/Getty Images.

Printed in the United States of America

CPSIA compliance information: Batch #CS11GS: For further information contact Gareth Stevens, New York, New York at 1-800-542-2595.

Contents

- -

Contenido

Boldface words appear in the glossary/
Las palabras en **negrita** aparecen en el glosario

No Spitting!

Spitting cobras are a group of snakes that can shoot **venom** from their **fangs**. They don't do this when they're hunting for food. They only do it to chase away enemies. The venom hurts when it hits an animal in the eyes.

¡Prohibido escupir!

La cobra escupidora pertenece a un grupo de serpientes que puede escupir **veneno** desde sus **colmillos**. Las escupidoras no hacen esto cuando cazan para comer. Sólo escupen para alejar a sus enemigos. El veneno afecta los ojos de los otros animales.

5

Spitting Cobras of the World

Spitting cobras live in hot areas of Africa, Asia, and Australia. They're found in grasslands, plains, and rocky hillsides. The longest type of these snakes is called Ashe's spitting cobra. It can grow to more than 9 feet (2.7 m) long!

- -

Cobras escupidoras en el mundo

Las cobras escupidoras viven en áreas calientes de África, Asia y Australia. Las escupidoras viven en prados, praderas y en laderas rocosas. La cobra escupidora de Ashe, o gigante, es la más grande de estas serpientes. ¡Puede medir más de 9 pies (2.7 m) de largo!

7

Different and the Same

Spitting cobras can be different sizes and colors. Like all cobras, spitting cobras can make the part of their body just below their head wider and flatter. This is called a hood. A cobra's hood makes it look bigger and scarier to its enemies.

Parecidos y diferencias

La cobra escupidora puede tener diferentes tamaños y colores. Al igual que otras cobras, las escupidoras pueden hacer una parte de su cuerpo, por debajo de la cabeza, más ancha y plana. A esto se le llama caperuza. La caperuza de la cobra la hace parecer más grande y peligrosa.

9

Growing Up

Spitting cobras lay eggs in old logs, **termite** nests, and animal **burrows**. Babies are venomous and start hunting right away. While adults hunt mainly at night, young snakes often hunt during the day. Spitting cobras eat small animals, such as lizards, frogs, and mice.

Crecimiento

La cobra escupidora pone sus huevos en viejos troncos, nidos de **termitas** y en las **madrigueras** de otros animales. Los bebés son venenosos y comienzan a cazar de recién nacidos. Las adultas cazan principalmente de noche, pero las serpientes jóvenes cazan durante el día. La cobra escupidora come lagartos, ranas, ratones y otros animales pequeños.

11

Spitting or Spraying?

Spitting cobras don't actually spit their venom. They spray it! The venom is stored in small body parts called glands. The cobras use **muscles** around these glands to push the venom out through holes in their fangs.

- -

¿Escupir o rociar?

Las cobras escupidoras no "escupen" el veneno. ¡Lo rocían! El veneno se encuentra en recipientes dentro del cuerpo llamadas glándulas. Las escupidoras usan los **músculos** alrededor de la glándula para empujar el veneno a través de los agujeros de sus colmillos.

13

Hit the Target

Some spitting cobras can spray their venom up to 10 feet (3 m) away! They're very good at hitting small **targets**. The cobra commonly aims for its enemy's eyes. The venom causes pain and blinds the enemy. This lets the cobra escape.

- -

En el blanco

!Algunas cobras escupidoras pueden rociar veneno a 10 pies (3 m) de distancia! Además son muy hábiles para dar en **blancos** pequeños. Generalmente la cobra apunta a los ojos del enemigo. El veneno provoca dolor y la víctima no puede ver. Así, la cobra logra escapar.

15

Deadly Bite

The venom a spitting cobra sprays isn't meant to cause death. However, the snakes do use their venom to kill **prey**. Spitting cobras shoot their venom into prey by biting them. Their fangs are short, but they're sharp enough to break through the animal's skin.

- -

Mordida mortal

El veneno que una cobra escupidora rocía no es mortal. Sin embargo, las cobras usan el veneno para matar a sus **presas**. Las cobras escupidoras transmiten el veneno al morder a la presa. Sus colmillos son cortos, pero lo suficientemente filosos como para penetrar la piel de los animales.

17

Spitting Cobras and People

People sometimes scare spitting cobras when walking in the wild. It takes just a few seconds for a spitting cobra to spray venom into a person's eyes. The venom can cause blindness if the person doesn't wash it out of their eyes right away.

La cobra escupidora y las personas

En ocasiones, la gente asusta a la cobra escupidora. Bastan unos segundos para que la cobra rocíe su veneno en los ojos de una persona. Si la persona no se lava los ojos de inmediato puede perder la vista.

19

The Mozambique Spitting Cobra

The Mozambique spitting cobra is one of the deadliest snakes in Africa. It can raise up to two-thirds of its body off the ground. It spreads its hood to look scarier. This snake can hit an animal's eyes from 8 feet (2.4 m) away.

La cobra escupidora de Mozambique

Una de las serpientes más mortales de África es la cobra escupidora de Mozambique. Esta serpiente puede levantar dos terceras partes de su cuerpo. Cuando abre su capucha da mucho miedo. Esta serpiente puede rociar veneno en los ojos de un animal a 8 pies (2.4 m) de distancia.

Snake Facts/
Hoja informativa

Mozambique spitting cobra/
Cobra escupidora de Mozambique

Length/Longitud	up to 4 feet (1.2 m) hasta 4 pies (1.2 m)
Color/Color	green-gray, brown, or gray and black verde-grisácea, marrón, o girs y negra
Where It Lives/ Hábitat	southern Africa sur de África
Eggs/Huevos	Females can lay up to 22 eggs at one time. Las hembras pueden poner hasta 22 huevos.
Killer Fact/ Datos mortales	The Mozambique spitting cobra is easily angered. However, it's known to play dead when facing larger enemies. La cobra escupidora de Mozambique se molesta fácilmente. Pero, se sabe que juega al muerto cuando enfrenta animales más grandes.

Glossary/Glosario

burrow: an animal home dug into the ground

fang: a long, sharp tooth

muscle: a body part that helps an animal move

prey: an animal hunted by another animal

target: an object to aim at

termite: a small bug that lives in large groups and eats wood

venom: something a snake makes inside its body that can harm other animals

- -

blanco (el) un objetivo

colmillo (el) un diente, largo y filoso

madriguera (la) el hogar que un animal excava en el terreno

músculo (el) la parte del cuerpo que ayuda a que se mueva un animal

presa (la) un animal cazado por otro animal

termita (la) un insecto pequeño que vive en grupos grandes y come madera

veneno (el) sustancia que producen las serpientes con la que pueden hacer daño a otros animales

For More Information/Más información

Books/Libros

Kopp, Megan. *Cobras*. Mankato, MN: Capstone Press, 2011.

Roza, Greg. *Poison! The Spitting Cobra and Other Venomous Animals.* New York, NY: PowerKids Press, 2011.

Websites/Páginas en Internet

The Crocodile Hunter Diaries: Spitting Cobra

animal.discovery.com/videos/the-crocodile-hunter-diaries-spitting-cobra.html
Watch crocodile hunter Steve Irwin get attacked by a spitting cobra.

Fooled by Nature: Spitting Cobra

videos.howstuffworks.com/animal-planet/28417-fooled-by-nature-spitting-cobra-video.htm
Watch a video of a spitting cobra spraying venom at an enemy.

Reptiles: Cobra

www.sandiegozoo.org/animalbytes/t-cobra.html
Learn more about cobras, including spitting cobras.

Index/Índice